INVENTIONS & EXTENSIONS

High-Interest, Creative-Thinking Activities

by Geri Blond & Doris Spivack

Incentive Publications, Inc.
Nashville, Tennessee

*Author proceeds donated to the
Geri Blond Memorial Fund for Early Intervention
at the Maple Center, Beverly Hills, California.*

Cover and illustrations by Susan Eaddy
Edited by Sherri Y. Lewis

ISBN 0-86530-209-X

TABLE OF CONTENTS

ENTERPRISING INVENTIONS

INTRODUCTION

Have your students ever asked you, "Who invented the Toll House cookie?" or "Why did Mr. Noah Webster invent the dictionary?"

This resource contains the history of inventors and their inventions that should spark interest in history and motivate your students to become involved in critical thinking projects.

An easy-to-understand and interestingly written information base about each invention and inventor is preceded by motivational questions sure to capture and hold students' interest. Also included are extensions following each invention which help you take the learning process one step further. Your students can create inventions similar to the ones they are learning about or participate in enrichment activities that relate to the invention. One of the suggested extensions related to the question, "What were some of the earliest musical instruments?" encourages students to invent original musical instruments from recycled materials.

A materials-needed list is also included with emphasis placed on using recycled materials which might otherwise become household throwaways.

The bibliography has been developed to encourage students to find out more about their favorite inventions and for use as an easy reference to help you develop the additional lessons focusing on inventions and extensions that your students are sure to demand.

How To Start

GETTING STARTED

1. Set up a table with: roll of tape, light bulb, pencil, tennis ball, comb, small radio, roll of film, battery, etc. (Try to have at least ten to twelve objects.)

2. Ask the students: "Why is this collection here? What do all of these objects have in common?" (Answer: They are all inventions.)

3. What are some things that are **not** inventions? (Answer: air, fire, water, trees, mountains, oceans.)

4. Who can be an inventor? (Answer: Anyone who has an idea.)

5. Why do people invent things? (Answers: To make the world better; to make life easier; to make money.)

6. **Activity**: Let the class take turns naming their favorite invention. (Example: Television. When something is named, it cannot be repeated by another student; each student should name a different invention.)

PLAY "Remember."

Student #1 says, "Film."
Student #2 says, "Tissue paper."
Student #3 says, "Football."
Student #4 says, "Scissors."

Then student #5 must repeat all four inventions and add a new one of his own. Try three inventions with first graders, five with second graders, and eight to ten with third graders.

IDEAS, IDEAS

Brainstorming is an exercise in thinking. Inventing is a combination of brains and materials. The more brains you use, the less materials you should need! Here is a way to help you use brain power!

1. Select an object such as a broom, picture frame, wire, electric cord, toothbrush, pencil, or any invention.

2. Ask the class to think of as many different ways as possible to use this invention. (Example: Other ways to use a **toothbrush** – Christmas tree decoration, eyebrows for a puppet, doghouse fence.)

3. There should be no judgmental remarks. There are no right or wrong, good or bad ideas. Spontaneous, creative answers should be encouraged.

4. Record all the ideas. Often, one idea leads to another.

5. **Writing Experience**: Let students choose one or a combination of some of the brainstormed inventions. Let them write short stories with illustrations about their chosen inventions.

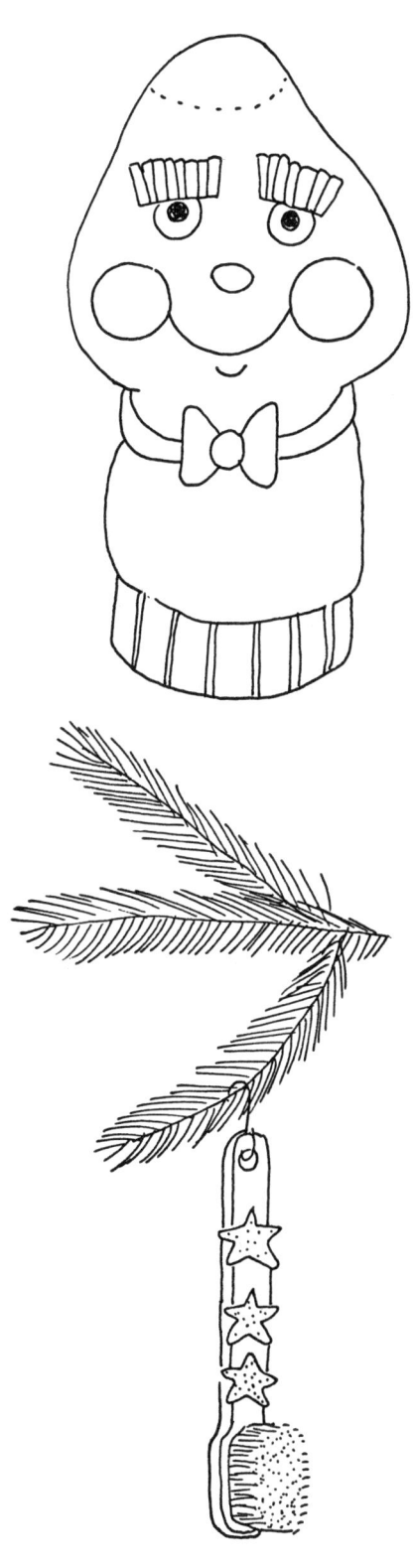

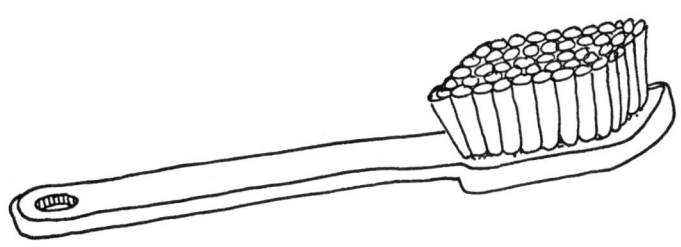

WHY RECYCLE?

By throwing away solid waste, we have created a huge garbage and rubbish disposal problem in the United States and in other countries around the world. Although we have systems to dispose of our trash through city dumps, by incineration, or other means, none of these methods can cope with the enormous amount of rubbish produced today. Garbage pollutes our land, sea, and air.

There are important ways students can improve our solid waste problem:

• REDUCE: Save writing paper partially used. Write on both sides of paper. Use cloth rags instead of paper towels.

• REUSE: Save wrapping paper and ribbon. Use a lunch bag more than one day. Reuse plastic bags.

• RECYCLE: Save materials for creative projects. (A list is included on page 12.)

Students should enjoy learning ways to **reduce**, **reuse**, and **recycle**. They may want to add their ideas to these examples. Materials are easy to find (**paper** and **paper products**, all types of **aluminum**, most types of **glass**). Find out where **recycle centers** are located in your community and visit them.

(Most of the creative projects in *Inventions & Extensions* utilize recycled materials.)

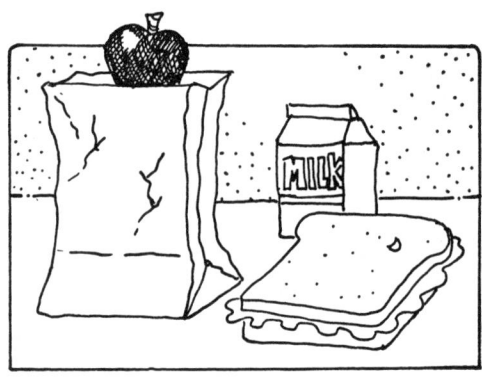

"Recipes" For Recycled Materials

For Recycled Paper:

Materials: Newspaper, buckets or bowls, water, hand beater, pieces of screen or felt

Procedure: For each piece of finished, recycled paper, tear a half page of newspaper into 1/2 inch to 1 inch pieces. Fill bowls with one part paper pieces and two parts water. Let the paper pieces soak overnight. Food coloring or beet juice can be added for color. Use a hand beater to "pulp" the fibers in the paper. Beat the mixture until it looks like mush. Take a handful of pulp and place it on a piece of screen or felt. Mold the pulp to the size of the sheet of paper you want to make. Press out excess water with hands or rolling pin. Let the paper dry one to two days. Remove it from the screen, and your paper is ready!

For Compost:

Materials: Large glass bowl or jar; vegetable, fruit, and bread scraps; soil

Procedure: Layer damp earth and chopped scraps. Dampen and add food scraps to the mixture daily for two weeks. Note the progression of the decaying food scraps. Plant a class garden in the jar!

Collage:

Materials: Pictures of recycled items from magazines; white glue or rubber cement; some small items such as straws, feathers, buttons, etc.; cardboard or mat board

Procedure: Glue the pictures and items to cover the cardboard or mat board. This can be used as an individual or class project.

Recycled Materials For Your Invention Corner

- paper
  (construction, tissue, wrapping, foil)

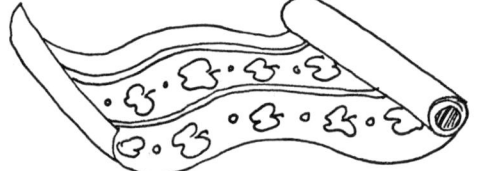

- wallpaper samples

- empty paper towel &
  toilet paper cardboard rolls

- screws, springs, pipes

- cotton balls & swabs

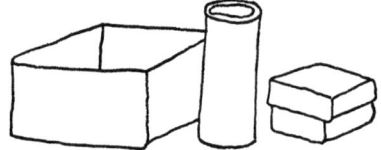

- cardboard containers

- cup lids

- doweling, moldings

- computer parts and cards

- automotive parts

- colored telephone wire

- foam rubber

- glue, paste, tape

- crayons & markers

- mailing tubes

- straws

- styrofoam plates, pieces, balls

- brown bags

- old greeting cards

- nuts, bolts

- watch, radio, & TV parts

- tongue depressors & orange sticks

- plastic spoons & glasses

- plastic film canisters

- plastic & ceramic flowerpots

- shells & stones

- old game pieces & parts

- fabric, ribbon, lace, fringe

- egg cartons, boxes, berry baskets

- nails, brads, staples

- uncooked pasta (unusual shapes)

- juice cans

- clothespins

INVENTOR'S CORNER

Ask students to bring materials that can be recycled to class (see list on previous page). The more variety, the more creative the corner will be. Make a chart with these following six items to display to the class.

1. Think about what you want to make.
2. Think about what it will look like and how it will work.
3. Select only the materials you will need to use.
4. Invent, create, enjoy!
5. Write a story about your invention.
6. Clean up, please!

THREE TABLES FOR THE INVENTION CORNER:

A. Building, drawing, and writing materials

B. A worktable only

C. To display inventions

STUDENTS CAN:

1. Students can work at the Invention Corner during free or assigned time.

2. They can work individually or in groups*.

3. They can share their ideas orally with the class and demonstrate what they invent.

4. Inventions can be displayed at an open house or shared with another class.

   * Planning and creating an invention provides an excellent opportunity for students to work cooperatively.

The whole class can develop inventions at the same time. You may wish to assign classroom groups with mixed levels of students including some from each – top, middle, low, and creative, etc., in one group.

Teacher's directions should include a **category** of inventions to problem-solve, i.e., invent a new method to recycle waste, walk the dog, carry homework, or paint a house.

Direct the students to discuss their invention in their groups. They should discuss the need for the idea, what it will look like, and how it will work.

Then working cooperatively, have the students select materials to construct or draw their invention. An oral presentation culminates this activity. It is ideal if all the group members can participate. The explanation should carefully explain the purpose of the invention and how the group reaches a decision.

TAKE A SURVEY

How can you decide which inventions will improve our world?

1. Think of these inventions by yourself.

2. Ask other people. Take surveys and let each person vote for two inventions. (Suggestions: air pollution, education, space travel, earth travel, games, toys, medicine, TV, film, video, etc.)

Tally your votes. Which invention is most needed according to your survey? Which invention came in second place? Third?

Invention Alphabet

One day, the letters of the alphabet had a meeting. All twenty-six were there. **A** was the first to speak.

"My life is always the same," he said. "The alphabet starts with my letter, and children will say **A is for anteater** or **antelope** when they think of me."

"You're right," said **B**. "**B is for butterfly** or **bullfrog**. How boring!"

"**C** is for **cow**. That is not very creative," chimed **C**.

"Not to mention **D** for **deer** and **E** for **elephant**," added **D** and **E**.

"I have an idea," said **I**, who usually had good ideas. "Why should our alphabet be about animals? Animals are nice, that's true. But they're not clever or **inspiring** or even very **interesting**! (**I** likes to use "I" words when he speaks.) Let's make up an invention alphabet."

"Great idea!" cried the letters. "We'll ask the children to think of an invention for each letter."

"But remember," said **B**, "they must be aware that some things won't belong in the invention alphabet." (Things that are not inventions and should not be included are: air, water, mountains, trees, grass, rocks, sunlight, rain, animals, birds, etc.)

"Is it fair to use a dictionary?" asked **D** who was disturbed about this.

"Of course," said the letters, "a dictionary is definitely desirable!"

"All right," said **A**. "I'll begin..."

1. Ask for answers. Name inventions that begin with letters of the alphabet. Examples: **A** – airplane, anchor, arch; **B** – bicycle, bathtub, belt; **C** – clock, chair, chopsticks.

2. Write each letter on a small piece of paper and put it into a bag. Let students reach in the "grab bag" to select a letter. Illustrate with crayons or markers.

3. Assemble an invention alphabet display.

4. Older students may try playing charades with the letter assigned. Example: **B** for buttons; **Z** for zipper. The class should try to guess the invention as the student acts it out.

5. Use the dictionary. It will be helpful for thinking of inventions that begin with difficult letters such as **k, o, u**, etc.

A "WACKYDOODLE" INVENTION

This is a creative listening lesson that incorporates the invention theme and drawing, too!

TEACHER SAYS:

Today we will draw a "wackydoodle" invention! Pay careful attention to everything I say.

I will tell you all about the "wackydoodle" invention. It will have lots of parts and details, so you must listen very carefully. I will not repeat anything! You may not touch your crayon until I am finished. Do your own work. Do not look at anyone else's.

There will be a time limit.

Do not talk.

Do not ask any questions.

WACKYDOODLE DESCRIPTION:

It has:

a rectangular body,

two squares and a triangle on top of the body,

two large circles and four smaller circles on the body,

springs sticking out of one side,

three control knobs on the other side.

It is on two wheels.

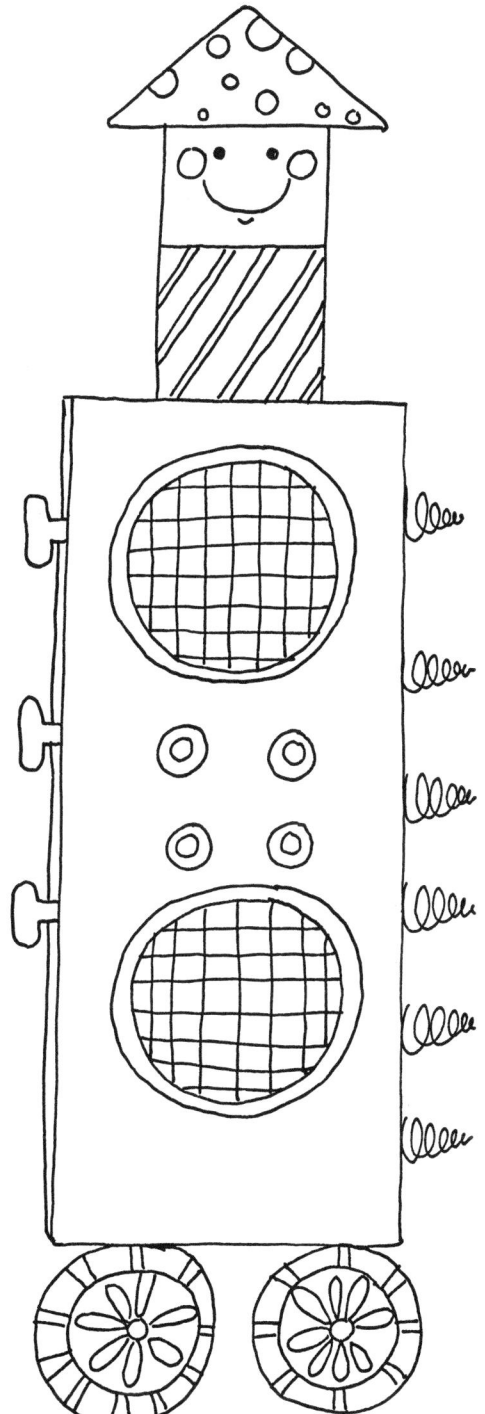

EXTENSION:

Give each student a 9" x 12" piece of paper. Tell students to use the paper vertically. Let each student choose one color of crayon to use except yellow. Allow students to draw for about 10 minutes. Then review the illustrations and see how well the students listened to your instructions.

FEELINGS

Can you invent feeling or only create a feeling?

INVENTION

You can invent a way to make yourself or a friend FEEL BETTER! Haven't you ever wished you had something special to cuddle when your feelings were hurt? Or something to squeeze or punch when something made you angry? Toy manufacturers are always looking for new inventions to make people feel good. So think about what it's like when your mood is "down" and how you would like to express yourself.

EXTENSIONS:

1. Use colored magic markers and draw on a white pillowcase. Draw things that make you feel good and that would make you forget what it was that made you feel bad.

2. Design a box full of things to make you feel good. What will you put in your box? Would this be a nice gift to take to a sick friend?

COMMUNICATION

WORDS

Can you name two of the most popular books ever printed in English? (The Bible *and* Webster's Dictionary.*)*

INVENTION

Noah Webster wrote the dictionary. He invented better ways to spell words and recognized the need for a book with all the words we use in it.

Noah was a teacher. He opened his own school and also earned a law degree. Noah was concerned that most all American schoolbooks were written in England and were not written the way Americans talked. So, Noah decided he would teach Americans to read and spell by writing an American spelling book.

His first spellers sold for 14 cents each and were covered in blue paper. Noah changed many words to make them easier to learn – "colour" to "color," "musick" to "music." In 1786 he met with Benjamin Franklin to talk about the difficulty with the American ways of spelling. He wanted to change "rough" to "ruff" and "tough" to "tuff," but no one would accept these ideas or others.

Noah rewrote his speller many times to improve and update it. He began a magazine in which he wrote articles about education and politics. He said that the first job of a government should be the education of its children.

EXTENSIONS:

1. Have a class spelling bee.

2. See how many words students can make from the word "dictionary."

3. See how many different words students can make from the letters in an alphabet breakfast cereal. Have them "write" a short story from the cereal.

WORD GAMES

Do you know when word games first started?

INVENTION

The popular Scrabble. game was invented by Alfred M. Butts, a New York City architect, in 1948. He got his idea from playing the old game of Anagrams which was played as long ago as the Middle Ages! In Anagrams, the letters in a word or phrase are rearranged to form another phrase. (Example: "they see" becomes "the eyes.") Mr. Butts liked arranging letters so much that he designed Scrabble. (word combinations formed on a board with wooden letters). There are many Scrabble. clubs all over the world, and the game is available in every language!

EXTENSIONS:

1. Let students invent their own word games. Tell them to choose a theme. Will it be about animals, space travel, geography, things to eat? How will you keep score? What will you play with? Who will go first? What will you use to make your game?

2. Play "Chalkboard Relay" in your classroom. You will need two teams. A player from each team writes a word on the chalkboard. The next player writes another word. The object is to write a complete sentence, and the first team to do that wins.

3. Write an "acrostic." Here is an example:

   John is 9 years
   Old and likes baseball.
   Hitting is fun but he's
   Never hit a home run. (yet)

4. Play "Words In-A-Bag." Each student writes eight different nouns on eight different cards. Put the words into a bag. Pass the bag around the room, and let each student close his eyes and pick out six words. Then each student should use these six words in a short story. The rest of the class tries to guess the six words that the student picked out of the bag. Continue play until each student has read his short story.

TELEPHONE TALK

Did you know battery acid "aided" Alexander Graham Bell in inventing the telephone?

INVENTION

Alexander Graham Bell was an American scientist who invented the telephone. The telegraph was invented before Bell's time. Noises, music, and signals were sent over electrified wires. However, human speech had never before been sent by wire.

As a boy, Alexander became interested in speech and hearing problems. As a young man he taught at a school for deaf people and even started a school of his own. Alexander learned about electricity and experimented with tuning forks, coiled springs, and batteries. At first he carried out his experiments alone, but then he joined with a young mechanic named Thomas Watson. They discovered how to transmit sound by accident.

One day, Bell and Watson were working in the same building on different floors. Bell accidentally spilled battery acid on his trousers while they were each holding a telephone and called out, "Mr. Watson, come here. I want you." These were the first words sent by telephone! By the end of 1876, telephone conversations between New York and Boston were possible. In 1915 the first transcontinental telephone line linked the United States with Europe.

EXTENSION:

1. Have students invent ways to send sound to another person. (Let students draw or build their inventions in the Inventor's Corner.)

GREETING CARDS

Who invented the first greeting card?

INVENTION

In England, the first card was designed by John Horseley in 1843. The first card appeared in the United States in 1874 by Louis Prang. The Hallmark Corp. has a collection of many early cards. When greeting cards first surfaced, some people thought the idea of sending cards was foolish and expensive. The cards were delivered by messengers on horseback. Today, several billion cards are sent at Christmastime and for other occasions throughout the year.

EXTENSIONS:

1. Have students invent their own greeting cards. Encourage them to use different shapes. Give them paper and other materials to draw and/or construct their cards. Then construct mobiles out of their handmade cards.

2. Have students make a list of reasons for sending cards.

LEONARDO

What do the parachute and "The Mona Lisa" have in common?

INVENTION

Leonardo da Vinci was born in 1452, lived in Italy, and was a genius in almost all the arts and sciences. He tried to learn how birds fly. He drew plans for flying machines and bicycles long before they were invented. The airplane, helicopter, tank, submarine, and parachute were all Leonardo's ideas even though they did not exist while he was alive. Leonardo kept notebooks filled with writings and drawings of his many ideas.

His two most famous paintings were "The Mona Lisa" and "The Last Supper." "The Mona Lisa" is an oil painting on wood and usually hangs in the Louvre, a museum in Paris, France. "The Last Supper" is a fresco which is in a monastery in Milan, Italy.

EXTENSIONS:

1. Have students draw a picture of their family at supper.

2. Have students write a story about why they think "The Mona Lisa" is smiling.

3. Once Leonardo invented a machine to tip a lazy student out of bed in the morning. Ask students to invent an alarm to wake them up for school.

4. Leonardo dreamed of underground travel. Ask students what they can invent to travel underground. How will they breathe?

PHOTOS

Did you know who invented the first camera and how the first color film was developed?

INVENTION

The camera was invented by a Frenchman named Louis Daguerre in 1839. Years later, in 1888, George Eastman named his camera invention the Kodak (because he especially liked the letter "K"), and he called his company Eastman Kodak.

The first film made black and white pictures or prints. Then in 1942 Leo Mannes and Leo Godowsky came to work for Eastman Kodak. They said that they could invent color film. They were musicians as well as inventors. While they worked, they liked to sing, but they sang to time the chemical reactions on the film. (Remember, there are no lights in a darkroom, and it must be absolutely dark for film to develop properly.) Today, there are electronic devices for that job.

EXTENSIONS:

1. Have students bring some color and black and white prints to share with the rest of the class.

2. Write a letter from the class to: The Eastman Kodak Company, 800 Lee Road, Rochester, New York 14650. Ask for information about the history of the company and what new products they are currently working on.

3. Let students use one or more film canisters to invent a game, toy, something to hold small objects, hanging decorations, etc. Let them share their inventions with the rest of the class.

Music Makes The World Go Round

What were some of the earliest musical instruments?

INVENTION

Early in Egyptian history, people clapped disks and sticks together, jingled metal rods, and sang songs. Their army used drums and trumpets.

In Jerusalem, stringed instruments such as harps were played in the temples.

The Chinese believed that music had magical powers, and their musicians played the flute, zither, and percussion instruments.

In Italy, music dates back to ancient times when wind, string, and keyboards were played.

The Greeks used letters of the alphabet to represent musical notes. Music was important in dance, drama, and religion.

Music can be beautiful to listen to or to learn to play. The categories of instruments are: stringed, woodwind, brass, and percussion.

EXTENSIONS:

1. Ask students what kinds of musical instruments they can invent using recycled materials. Here are some ideas:

   A. Make a drum using empty oatmeal boxes.

   B. Make "finger" cymbals by attaching bottle caps, buttons, or large coins to your fingers with rubber bands.

   C. String some small bells together.

   D. Make a "mover and a shaker." Fill juice cans with rice, beans, marbles, or dried peas.

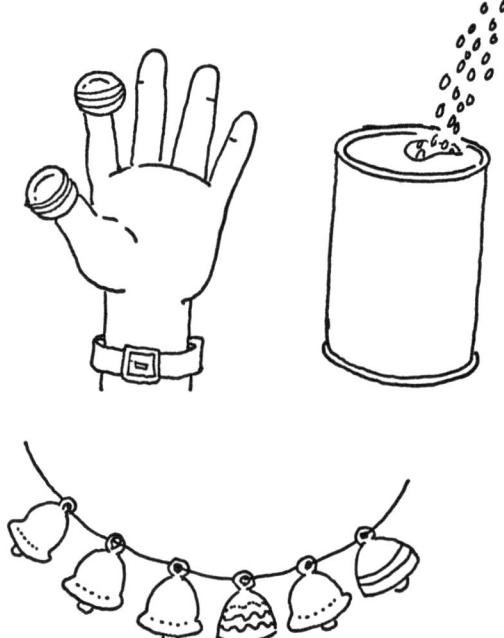

CIRCLES

What do doughnuts and golf have in common? (Holes.)

INVENTION

In 1698, a sea captain named Hanson Gregory was steering his ship while eating a fried cake. The weather suddenly became stormy and the ship began to toss on the sea. Captain Gregory needed both of his hands to steer the ship, so he rammed the fried cake onto one of the spokes on the steering wheel. He was so impressed with the hole he made, he ordered the ship's cook to make the fried cakes with holes from then on – hence, doughnuts! Today, you can buy doughnut holes separately from doughnuts.

Golf: Although Scotland is the home of golf, it is not known exactly who invented the game. The first golf course was built in 1764 in St. Andrews, Scotland, and originally had twenty-two holes. Today, eighteen holes is the standard for a golf course.

EXTENSIONS:

1. Have students draw a circle on a piece of paper. Ask them to add smaller circles. Let them draw rabbits, mice, snowmen, or faces out of circles.

2. Invent a game using large, rubber washers. Let students throw an object into the washers and record their scores.

3. Let each student make a list of all the places they see circles or holes. Look at clothing, windows, tops of cans, etc.

Invent a Cookie

What do Ruth Wakefield and Wally Amos have in common?

INVENTION

Your sweet tooth can probably answer correctly. Each invented a delicious chocolate chip cookie!

Mrs. Wakefield of Lowell, Massachusetts, created the chocolate chip cookie by accident. In 1933 she was preparing a batch of chocolate butter drops. Instead of melting chocolate squares for the batter, she broke a semisweet candy bar into pieces and stirred it into the mix. She thought the chocolate chunks would melt in the heat of the oven. To her surprise, the chocolate stayed firm and the cookie tasted yummy! Wakefield named her invention the toll house cookie after the Toll House Inn which she and her husband Kenneth owned.

As the Toll House ® chocolate chip cookie grew in popularity, the Nestle Company began distributing chocolate morsels specifically for Mrs. Wakefield's recipes. More than 90 million bags of chocolate morsels are sold each year.

Wally Amos derived his "Famous Amos ®" cookie from the recipe created by Ruth Wakefield. Amos said he gave his personality to the recipe by adding more nuts and chips. Wally credits his Aunt Della as the first person who made cookies for him and inspired him to create his famous cookie.

As a teenager, Wally attended a New York City trade school and served an apprenticeship at a local hotel as a cook. After four years in the Air Force, he became a talent agent with the William Morris Agency. He passed out his chocolate chip cookies at meetings and on television and movie sets. Wally always looked for a superstar to represent his product, and in 1970 he found one...himself...thus the name the Famous Amos ® Chocolate Chip Cookie!

...INVENT A COOKIE

INVENTION cont.

Amos borrowed money from his showbusiness friends to start a cookie store. He worked 18 hours some days baking cookies, handling interviews, and talking about his product. He sometimes baked all night long. Soon Amos, his cookie, and his straw Panama hat and embroidered shirt, which he frequently wore, became celebrities.

Today, Wally Amos is a millionaire. He attributes his success to believing in himself and the fact he could sell chocolate chip cookies.

EXTENSIONS:

1. For more information about successful cookie makers, write:

   • The Famous Amos Chocolate
     Chip Cookie Corporation
     680 Knox Street
     P.O. Box 2908
     Torrance, California 90509

   • Mrs. Debbie Fields, Inc.
     333 Main Street, P.O. Box 4000
     Park City, Utah 84060

   • Nestle Foods Corporation
     Purchase, New York 10577
     1-800-553-5303

2. Let students study the recipe on the back of a package of Nestle Toll House® Morsels. Famous Amos changed Mrs. Wakefield's recipe. Let students change or add to this recipe to invent new kinds of cookies.

3. Let students design their own cookies or gingerbread men using chocolate or vanilla frosting, sprinkles, raisins, cinnamon hearts, etc. Use tongue depressors dipped in frosting to "paste" on the decorations for the face and body.

Peanuts And Potatoes

Did you know some shaving creams and shampoos contain peanut products?

INVENTION

George Washington Carver was born a son of slaves in 1860 in Missouri and grew up to be very famous in agriculture. He asked questions about plants that no person or book could answer. George experimented with plants and found "secrets" no one else knew.

He taught farmers in Alabama to rotate their crops to keep their land fertile. He is considered an inventor because he developed hundreds of different products from peanuts and sweet potatoes. Some of the sweet potato products are soap, coffee, and starch. Carver made over 300 different products from the peanut! (Here are a few peanut products students may not know: paper, ink, shaving cream, sauces, linoleum, shampoo, and milk.)

EXTENSIONS:

1. Tell students to mix peanut butter with other foods to see what they can make. Let them bring a sandwich to school for their lunch and share what is in their mixtures with the other students. (One suggestion might be a peanut butter, banana, and raisin sandwich.)

2. Let half the students put sweet potatoes in water-filled jars. Prop the sweet potatoes with toothpicks. Let the rest of the students plant peanuts in soil. Discuss why or why not the sweet potatoes and/or peanuts grow.

3. Let students plant radish seeds in berry baskets using different kinds of soil. Let them try potting soil, dirt, and sand. Discuss which soil is best for the seeds.

4. Carver said that a weed is a flower growing in the wrong place. Have students find weeds and flowers in their yard or a neighbor's and tell the class their names. Tell the students to bring samples if possible so the rest of the class can learn new weed and plant names, too.

FOR PEANUT BUTTER LOVERS

Where is the "peanut belt"?

INVENTION

Most Americans like peanut butter, but those that **really** love peanut butter may belong to a peanut butter lovers fan club! Americans spread peanut butter on bread for sandwiches; on crackers for snacks; or mix it with other ingredients to make cookies, cakes, sauces, and souffles.

Peanut butter was invented by a St. Louis doctor in 1890 as a protein substitute for elderly patients who had trouble chewing meat. The spread immediately became popular. Peanut butter is high in calories, 188 in two tablespoons, but it has no cholesterol. Peanut butter contains lots of vitamins, minerals, and fiber. As people learn more about natural foods, some say peanut butter is one of the best.

The nation's "peanut belt" is in Georgia, Alabama, and Florida.

EXTENSION:

1. Make this tasty recipe for students; then give them a copy to take home.

   1 pint vanilla ice cream
   1 cup chunky peanut butter

   Mix these two ingredients, and pour into a graham cracker pie crust. Freeze. (Pie can be topped with chocolate sauce before freezing, or the sauce can be put on top of the pie before serving.)

FLY AWHILE

• *How many of you have flown on an airplane?*   • *Did you ever wonder how it stays up in the air?*

INVENTION

Orville and Wilbur Wright became interested in flying by reading about a man named Otto Lilienthal who was famous for his gliders. The brothers built a six-foot wind tunnel and tested more than 200 models of wings. Then they invented, built, and flew the first powered airplane called "The Kitty Hawk" near a town named Kitty Hawk in North Carolina in 1903. The plane was made of wood, muslin cloth, and wire; it flew for only 12 seconds. Their next flight lasted 59 seconds and covered 852 feet.

The Wright Brothers worked in secrecy to safeguard anyone attempting to steal their ideas. Today, inventors obtain a patent (special, written permission) to make and sell an idea. The patent protects the inventor's rights and makes it illegal for anyone else to steal or copy his idea.

EXTENSIONS:

1. Let students make paper airplanes or gliders.

2. Have students draw pictures of a new kind of flying machine. Where will they fly it? Will they travel forward or backward in time? Let them share their pictures and ideas with the rest of the class.

3. Let them make a patent for their invention. Make sure they date it.

Auto And Assembly Lines

Did you know that the first automobiles were made in Europe and used steam engines to run?

INVENTION

The first automobiles were called "horseless carriages." Gasoline engines were invented soon after, and they were similar to the engines we use in modern automobiles today. However, these automobiles were built by hand and were very expensive. Only the truly rich people could afford them.

In America, businessmen began seeking ways to build the automobile more cheaply. That way they could sell more cars to more people and increase their profit.

In 1893 an inventor named Henry Ford built his first car. (He became interested in machinery at the age of 15 when he worked as a watch repairman.) He was the first to start mass production of automobiles by letting each worker build one part of the car, and then the conveyor belt would carry the automobile to the next worker. We call this "assembly-line-manufacturing." Each worker is specialized in a certain part of the car.

In 1908 Ford built his famous Model T called the "Tin Lizzie." The factory could produce 100 cars a day then!

EXTENSIONS:

1. Write to the Ford Motor Company in Detroit, Michigan. Find out more about the automobile invention and share this information with the class.

2. Have students write stories telling why we need cars.

3. Let students build a machine that moves. (Check the materials list on page 12.) Try pasta for spokes, lids for wheels, boxes for the body, etc.

4. Let students start a pretend business with an assembly line production. (Suggestions: lemonade, book, sandwich, or salad stand.)

CONTAINERS

• What determines the shape of things? • Why is a garbage can in the form it is? • Why do frozen juice cans look like cylinders? • Do flower vases have to be tall and thin? • Should picture frames always be rectangular, round, or square? • Think about containers; then decide how you can invent something better or better-looking to hold things.

INVENTION

An Italian artist-inventor named Nini Policappelli had the idea to make more attractive mailboxes. He decided that the usual mailbox in front of most houses was a boring, uncreative box. So he began to design special mailboxes for his friends. Some of his designs looked like their owners and were made of wood or metal. Some had moveable arms in which the mailman placed the mail. Some were constructed out of geometric shapes in all colors. Others were shaped like flowers, plants, cars, and boats – all according to the interests of their owners.

EXTENSION:

1. Ask students to invent containers. Encourage them to use a combination of shapes. (Suggestions: mailbox, house, trash can, vase, new bed, car, boat, bookcase, desk, letter holder, backpack, picture frame, cereal box, etc.) Explain the materials you will use. Describe its size and color(s).

FUN INVENTIONS

PUPPET SHOW

PLAYING CARDS

Who invented card playing?

INVENTION

Marco Polo introduced cards to Europe, and Christopher Columbus brought them to America in the 15th century. The French first used the 52 card deck. The designs represented historic figures – Charlemagne, king of hearts; Julius Caesar, king of diamonds; King David, king of spades; Alexander the Great, king of clubs. Popular card games include: Rummy, Bridge, Canasta, Go Fish, Old Maid, Famous Authors, and Concentration. Today, the United States Playing Card Co. produces 280,000 decks of cards a day at its main offices in Cincinnati, Ohio.

EXTENSION:

1. Have each student invent a card game! Cards can have: pictures of people, flowers, animals, numbers, words, code symbols, colors, etc. Or, have them build a house of cards.

CONCENTRATION

- Glue pieces of fabric onto playing cards or draw twenty-six designs. You need twenty-six different designs to have twenty-six pairs of cards.

- Lay out the cards in careful rows. Let the students study the cards. Then turn the cards over so that only the paper tops are seen.

- Each player turns over a card and tries to find the match. The winner is the one with the most pairs.

DOLLS

Did you know Barbie and Ken were named after real children?

INVENTION

The Barbie® doll was invented by Ruth Handler in 1959. She was vice president and later president of the Mattel Toy® Company in Los Angeles. She, her husband Elliot, and Harold Matson formed the company. Ruth named the doll Barbie after her daughter who preferred to play with teenage dolls instead of baby dolls. She loved to choose various fashion accessories like scarves, jewelry, shoes, purses, hats, etc. At that time, the more grownup dolls were only available as paper cutouts. Although people did not think Barbie® would sell, they were proven wrong when the Barbie® doll sold $500 million in the first eight years after its introduction. Later, Ken was introduced and named for the Handler's son Ken.

EXTENSIONS:

1. Let students make dolls of their own. Use a sock or nylon stocking for the body.

2. Let students make puppets. (See puppet pages – 38 - 39.)

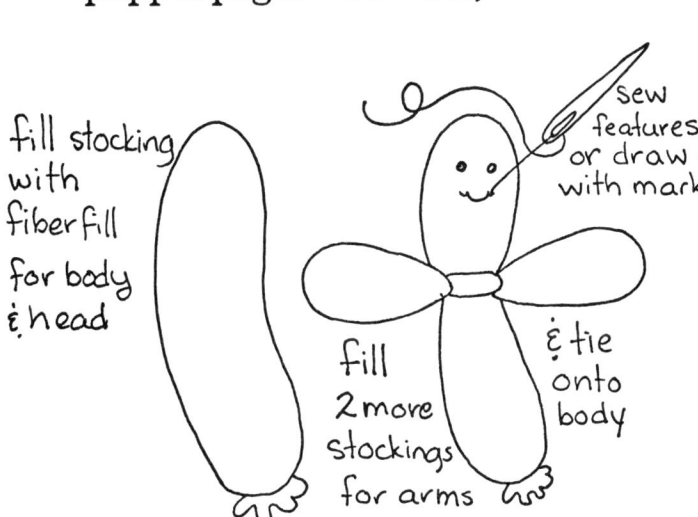

fill stocking with fiber fill for body & head

fill 2 more stockings for arms

sew features or draw on with markers

& tie onto body

sew on hair if you wish

37

PUPPETS

Can you think of any puppets on television today?

INVENTION

In Greek literature there are references to "string pullers" who may have been puppeteers or operators of puppet shows. Small puppets or dolls with a wire attached to the head have been found in ancient graves of children in Greece and Italy. American Indians used puppets, too.

The first puppet shows were about religion and morals. In many parts of Europe, puppet heroes were developed who spoke and acted like the people of the region. Later in America, children and adults who could not afford the regular theatre or lived too far away from it attended puppet shows. This continued until movies began.

In the 1900s a new kind of puppet show developed. Artists and writers wrote plays especially for puppets and made puppets that were works of art. The first "famous" puppets were Punch and Judy. The name Punch comes from Pulcinella, from Italy. Punch usually had a "fight" in the show. The Punch and Judy shows were written to teach a moral about right and wrong and were performed on city streets and parties.

You may be aware that puppets are used today in television programs and commercials. In the 1950s there was Kukla, Fran, and Ollie. (Fran was a real woman.) Howdy Doody, Paul Winchell's Jerry Mahoney, and Edgar Bergen's Charlie McCarthy were very well-known.

EXTENSION:

1. Have the students make puppets similar to the ones on the next page and/or encourage them to use their own ideas.

...PUPPETS

Match or Jewelry Box

Spoon

Clay & Dowels

Egghead

Construction Paper

PUSH-UP PUPPET

8" mailing tube

2" styrofoam ball

man's hi-top sock

tongue depressor for arms

16" dowel fits into ball

or oatmeal box cylinder

finished puppet moves freely

GO FLY A KITE

How did Benjamin Franklin's kite invention lead him to discover another invention?

INVENTION

You see Benjamin Franklin's face on stamps and money, and he also played an important part in America's history. He always seemed to have good ideas. Franklin invented a swimming machine and experimented with a kite to prove that lightning was electricity. The kite experiment helped him discover the idea of a lightning rod, a way to keep houses from catching on fire by lightning. This is still used today. (Ask students if they have ever seen one.)

Another of Franklin's famous inventions was the Franklin Stove. It fit into fireplaces and sent heat out into the room. This stove is still used today in many homes.

Ben Franklin seemed to have as many careers as ideas. He was an author, printer, businessman, inventor, scientist, ambassador, and statesman. Franklin was 84 years old when he died in 1790.

EXTENSIONS:

1. Have students design and build a kite. Then let them fly it at recess. Follow these steps:

   a. Build a frame in the shape of the illustration on the next page. Use light wooden sticks or dowels.

   b. Tie strings around edges of sticks.

   c. Glue light paper or plastic to the frame.

   d. Use strips of cloth for a tail.

2. Make a math kite! Write a number on the kite, and let students write various equations equal to that number on the kite bows. Let them use addition, multiplication, subtraction, or division problems.

3. Benjamin Franklin published a yearly magazine called *Poor Richard's Almanac*. It was famous for wise sayings such as, "Eat to live, not live to eat," and "Early to bed, early to rise, makes a man healthy, wealthy and wise." Have students look at the book in your library and then write their own sayings. Let them title their books with their own names, i.e., *Poor _____ (student's name) Almanac.*

4. Help students make up short plays using a moral from *Poor Richard's Almanac* as a theme. Establish plot, characters, and setting.

5. Benjamin Franklin was a newspaper publisher. Let students write stories for your school paper. Let them pretend they are Franklin working in a print shop while typing their papers.

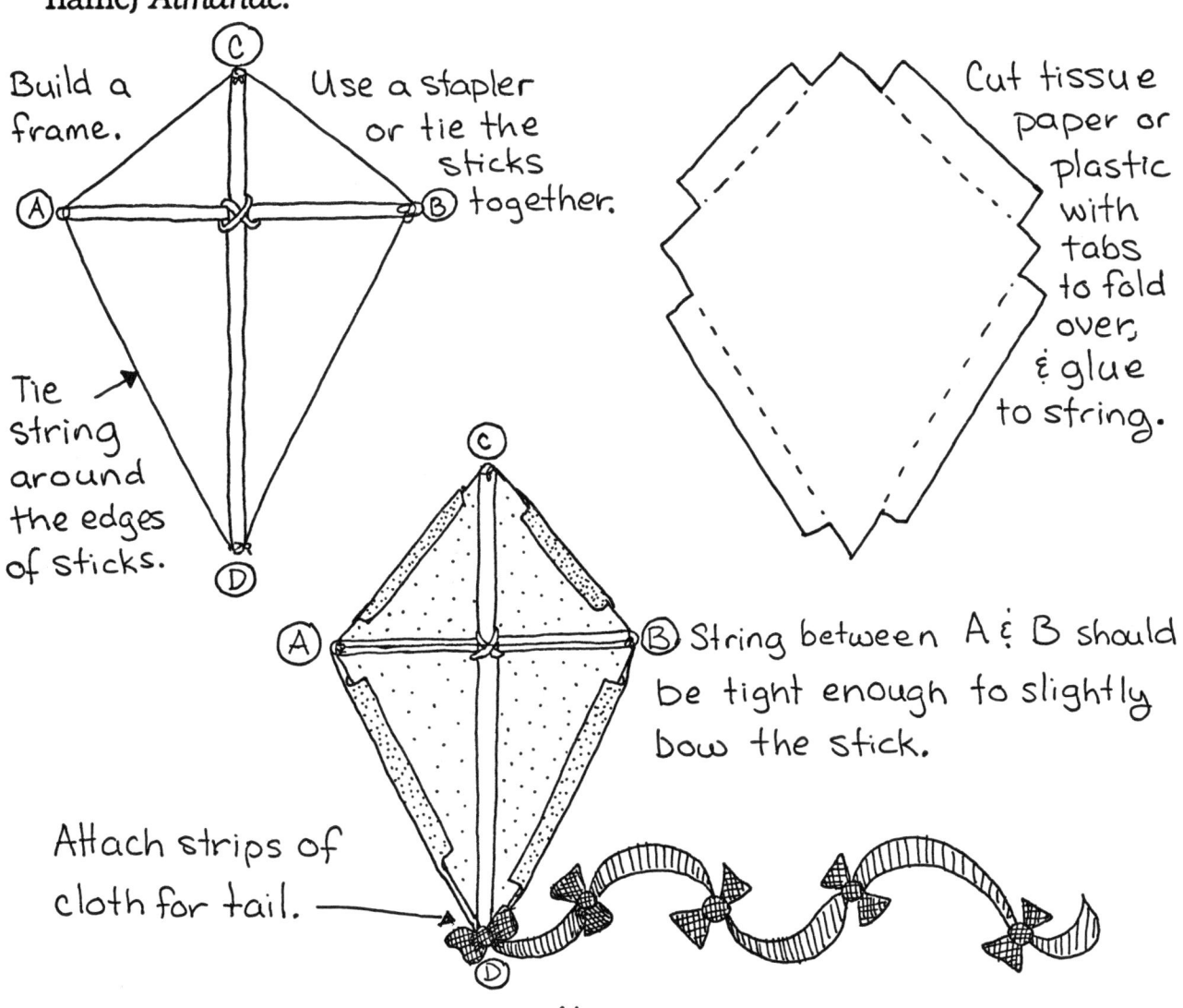

Build a frame.

Use a stapler or tie the sticks together.

Tie string around the edges of sticks.

Cut tissue paper or plastic with tabs to fold over, & glue to string.

String between A & B should be tight enough to slightly bow the stick.

Attach strips of cloth for tail.

THE OLDEST PUZZLE

Did you know a ceramic tile may have been the first puzzle?

INVENTION

According to legend, in ancient times a Chinese scholar had a favorite ceramic tile that he considered his greatest treasure. One day he was carrying it in his hands when he tripped. The tile smashed into seven pieces on the stone floor. The scholar spent the rest of his life trying to put the tile back together again. The puzzle was named "Tangram" since the scholar's name was Tan. This challenging invention includes only seven pieces, yet hundreds of interesting patterns and shapes can be created with them.

EXTENSIONS:

1. The youngest students can use the pieces freely to make designs. They should know the names of the geometric shapes – triangle, square, and rhomboid. The seven shapes form a perfect square. The possibilities are limitless for this puzzle – numbers, people, boats, planes, letters, cars, patterns, furniture, etc.

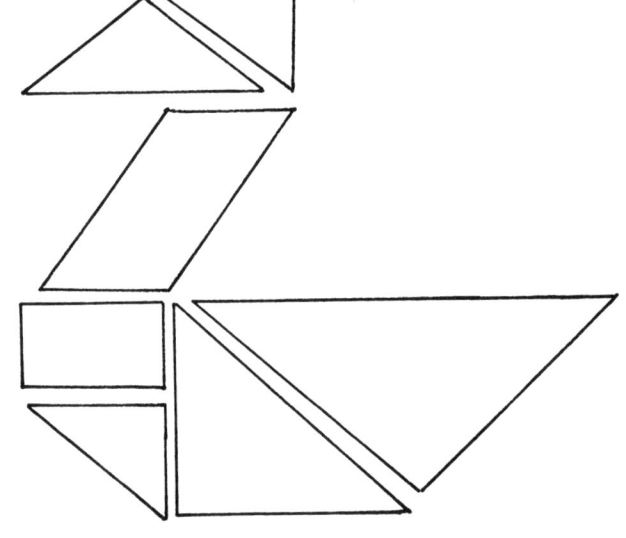

2. Students should try to put the pieces back together to form the square. This is challenging for all ages.

3. The Chinese name for the "Tangram" is "ch'i ch'iao t'u," meaning "ingenious seven-piece plan." Use the pattern on the next page to duplicate a puzzle for each student.

TANGRAM PATTERN

Cut each pattern out of a different color of construction paper. (Children can remember their color and avoid mixing puzzles.) When two or three puzzles are combined, interesting patterns can be formed.

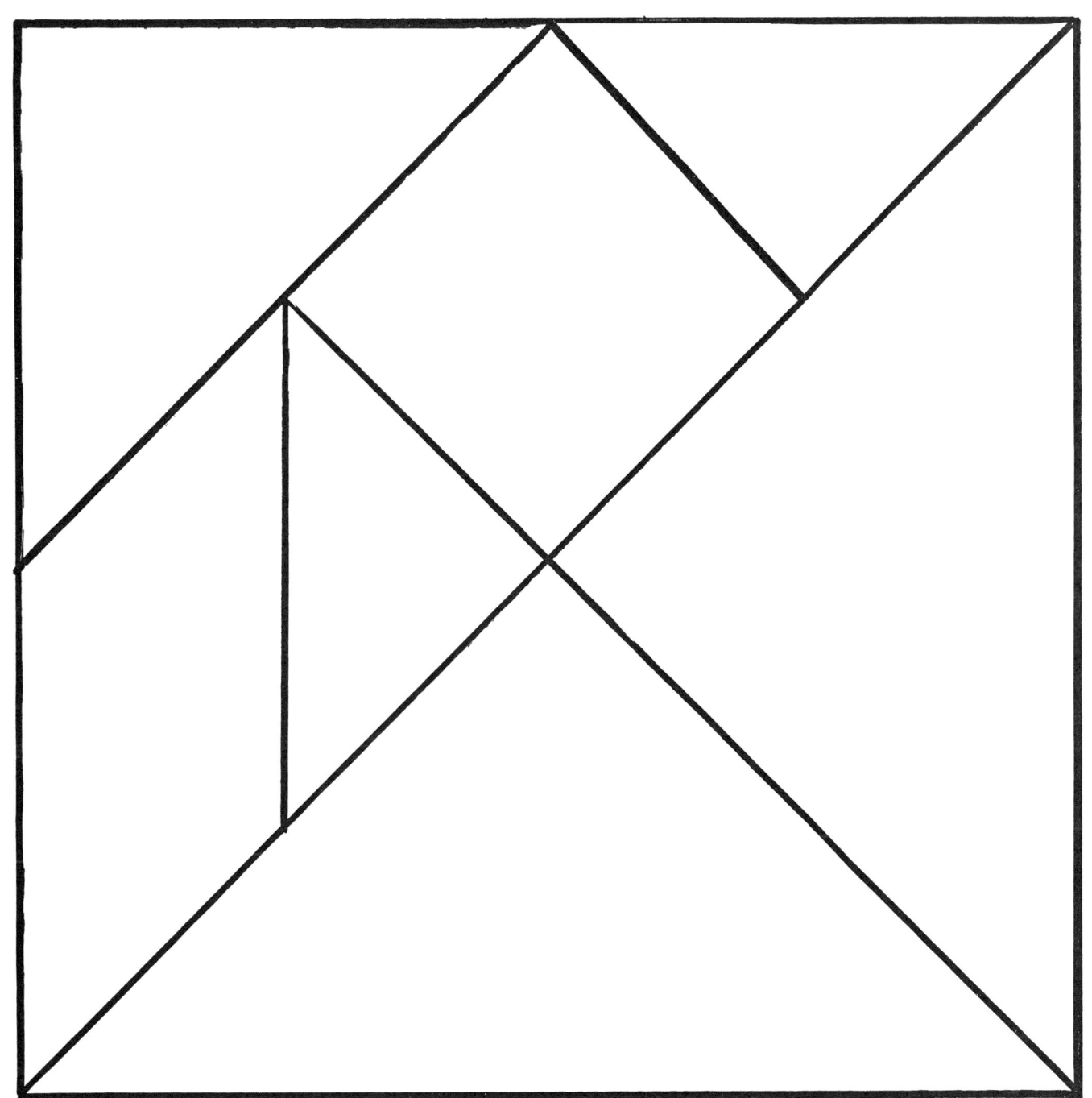

BUILDING

How old are Tinkertoys®?

─ INVENTION ─

Tinkertoys® were first introduced at the American Toy Fair in New York in 1913. Charles Pajeau, a stonemason from Evanston, Illinois, invented them. He was inspired by watching children play with sticks and empty spools of thread.

Building with Tinkertoys can be challenging and creative for all ages. In 1980, eight adults worked for 100 hours constructing a two-story fairy castle from 5,770 pieces.

Since 1978 the Philadelphia Franklin Institute of Science has hosted an annual Giant Tinkertoy® Extravaganza weekend. Costumed impersonators of famous inventors/tinkerers such as Benjamin Franklin, Leonardo da Vinci, and Alexander Graham Bell assist more than 16,000 children and adults including engineers, architects, and artists in building Tinkertoy® constructions.

Chemistry professors use them to make molecular models. Bell Telephone has used them to test management candidates, and Lockheed Corp. has used them for design models of planes.

Today, Tinkertoys® have plastic wheels and platforms.

Skyscrapers: Most skyscrapers are made of iron, steel, and glass today. Many years ago, houses were made of clay, wood, straw, and sometimes brick and stone.

In 1862, James Bogardus was the first American to build a high-rise department store. It stretched on New York's Broadway from 9th to 10th street, and it was eight stories high. He was so excited about his new iron building that he predicted buildings of the future would be miles high.

EXTENSIONS:

1. Let your students build with Tinkertoys® and share their creations with the class. Allow them to work in groups if you prefer.

...BUILDING

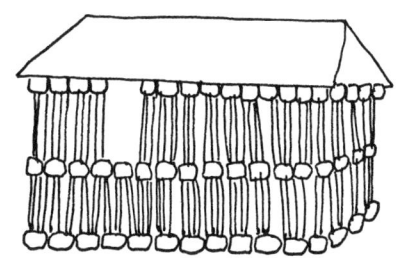

2. Have your students construct a building with film canisters, cups, playing cards, wood scraps, jewelry boxes, etc.

3. Bring ingredients for students to "build" sandwiches for lunch. Bring bread or rolls, meats, vegetables, fruits, seeds, nuts, etc. Let them draw pictures of their creations and then write recipes to take home.

4. Let students construct a building with miniature marshmallows and toothpicks. Use a box top or piece of cardboard as a base. Lay out a strong foundation of triangles. Build up carefully. Let students paint their building after it has dried.

5. Ask students to name some tall buildings in your city. How many different kinds can they name? Ask them how buildings differ in size and shape, what buildings are made of and who designs them, and how buildings are made strong.

LEGO® - ENDLESS POSSIBILITIES

How many combinations can you make with Legos®?

INVENTION

The Lego® brick was designed in 1949 by Ole Kirk Christiansen, a Danish carpenter and toy maker. He made small pieces of plastic and wood to interlock so children could build almost any structure they imagined.

The name is a contraction of "leg godt" which means "to play well" in Danish. In 1958, Ole's son Godtfred Kirk Christiansen patented the colored plastic bricks. It is said that two 8-stud bricks (of the same color) can be put together in twenty-four different ways. With six 8-stud bricks, the combination zooms to more than 100 million ways (102,981,500 to be exact – at last count!).

In 1961, Lego® introduced wheels, a Castle series, Light and Sound units, the town, dollhouse components, space equipment, and even a monorail.

The American division of the Lego® factory is located in Enfield, Connecticut, and is the size of ten football fields! The pieces are manufactured there in the six Lego® colors: red, yellow, blue, white, black, and gray.

Adults use Lego®, too. Architects in Great Britain hold an annual Lego® construction contest. Engineers in Montreal meet regularly to compare designs. There is even a Legoland park in Denmark!

EXTENSIONS:

1. Let students use Lego® bricks to build a city of the future, a figure or new form of transportation, an animal, or a spaceship. Or, they can be an architect and design a modern skyscraper. Students can work with a friend and connect their buildings.

2. Have students invent another building toy that fits together and has "clutch power" as Lego® does. Let them use: film canisters, small boxes, sticks, clay, macaroni, etc.

3. Let students participate in a classroom construction contest. Have judges award prizes for originality and quality of designs.

TOYS TO TOSS

Did you know a Frisbee® originated from a simple tin pie pan?

INVENTION

Throwing things for "sport" has always been popular. Cavemen tossed sticks, skipped stones on water, and rolled rocks. One game of "toss" began in the early 1900s in Bridgeport, Connecticut, where William Russell Frisbie owned and operated the Frisbie Pie Company. Pies were baked in 10-inch-wide tin pans. The empty-tin-catch game began and seemed to be fun.

In the late 1940s plastic was invented, and Walter Frederick Morrison decided that he could use this new material to invent a safer and lighter pie-tin game. It took a lot of experimenting to get the plastic just right for the new Frisbee® toy so it would not be too hard and break if it hit something or be too soft and melt in the sun.

Dogs can be trained to catch Frisbees®, and the newest disks are even battery-powered. A Frisbee® made out of foam can be played indoors, and one out of cloth can be folded up and put into a pocket.

EXTENSIONS:

1. Ask students to invent something that can be tossed in a game. How will you keep score? What materials will you use?

2. Ask students what they can invent that is made of plastic. They can use lids, film canisters, dishes, flat pieces, tubes, old notebooks, etc.

3. Make your toss game into a math game! The student who tosses gives a problem, e.g., "3 x 5." The student who catches must say the correct answer, or he is "out." (This could be a fun game to play in a circle.)

PLAY BALL!

• *How was football invented?*   • *Why was a ladder needed when basketball first began?*

INVENTION

Football began in the mid-1800s and was copied after soccer. The object was to kick a round ball across the other team's goal lines. Thirty or more players could be on a team. The first college football game was played in 1869 when Rutgers defeated Princeton 6-4. By 1900 the rules changed so that only eleven men could be on a team, and touchdowns started. In 1905 some colleges prohibited football because of frequent injuries. Players did not wear the protective shoulder and knee pads, helmets, and mouth guards they wear today.

Basketball: James A. Naismith, a physical education teacher, invented basketball in 1891. This was the first team sport that could be played indoors during the winter. Naismith wanted to make goals for his game, and the only thing he could find were wooden peach baskets. Basketball got its name from these baskets.

Each time a player scored, a ladder was brought onto the court to recover the ball. Eventually, metal baskets replaced the peach baskets, and they had a small hole in the bottom so the ball could be pushed out with a pole. In 1893 an inventive player created a trapdoor basket that released the ball by pulling on a cord. The bottomless net we have today was first used in 1913.

EXTENSION:

1. Let students invent a team sport ball game like football or basketball, or they can invent a board game to be played with a smaller ball.

ENTERPRISING INVENTIONS

BRAILLE

Do you know how Louis Braille became blind?

──── INVENTION ────

Louis Braille was born in Coupvray, France, in 1809. His father made harnesses and saddles out of fine leather. Louis promised he would never touch anything in the leather shop, but one day when Louis was 3 years old, he wandered into the workroom and picked up an awl, a sharp tool for making holes in leather. It slipped from his hand, and the point hit Louis in one eye. He was badly hurt, and an infection developed and spread to both eyes. At first Louis saw foggy shapes, then only blurs, and finally, Louis went blind.

But Louis enjoyed learning! At age seven he was accepted as the youngest student at the Royal Institute of Blind Youth in Paris. Louis studied hard and especially enjoyed learning to play the piano. The boys used canes to "tap-touch" their way around the school, and when they went into the city, they held onto a long rope and called themselves "the rope gang."

By 1820 Louis had learned to read slowly from a book with raised letters. Some of the letters were easy to feel, but it was difficult to tell the difference between the "C," "O," and "Q." "I's" could be "T's," and "R's" could be "B's." Other books for the blind were made with letters out of wood, wax, or even pins! Louis decided to invent a better way to make books for the blind.

In 1821 Louis met Captain Charles Barbier. The captain told of his "night writing" raised dots method so that soldiers could send messages in the dark. A word was broken down into a pattern of sounds. (It might take 100 dots to write one word!) The dots were punched into paper with a pointed tool called a stylus. This gave Louis an idea! He invented a six-dot cell that looked like this:

$$
\begin{array}{ll}
1\ \bullet & \bullet\ 4 \\
2\ \bullet & \bullet\ 5 \\
3\ \bullet & \bullet\ 6
\end{array}
$$

INVENTION cont.

Louis was excited. He knew his dot alphabet would work! He struggled for years to find people interested in his work. Braille taught at the institute and kept practicing the piano and making his dot books.

Finally in 1847, the first Braille printing press ended the old, slow way of making all the dots by hand. By 1900 every school for the blind was using Braille's invention. Now, blind people worldwide can read books due mostly to Louis Braille.

EXTENSIONS:

1. Write or call The Braille Institute in your city. Ask for information on books and materials for the blind. Share this information with your students.

2. Let students invent different games or toys for the blind. Make sure they use a variety of different textures.

3. Students can make their own braille alphabets. Give them dried split peas to glue on their papers.

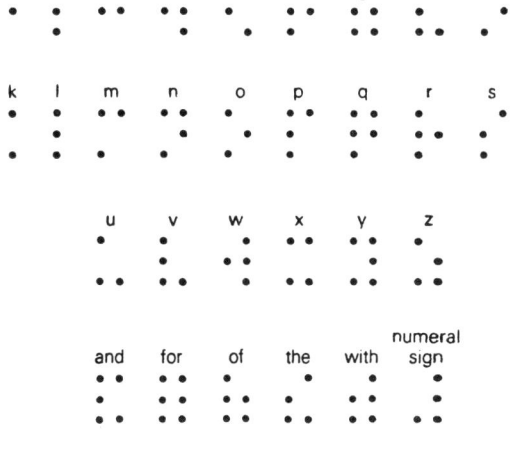

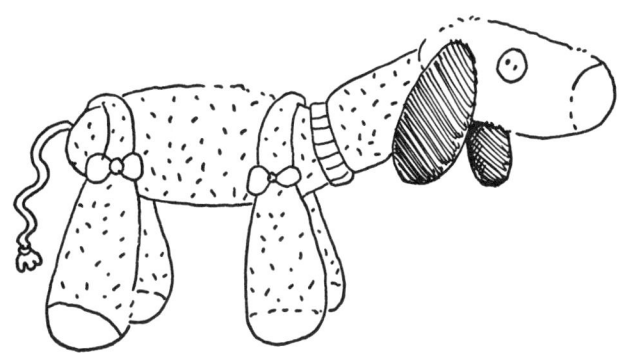

INVENTIONS FOR THE HANDICAPPED

Did you know there are hearing aids for pets?

— INVENTION —

Physically handicapped persons and animals are in constant need of new products. About one out of seven people in the world has some kind of disability. Often an invention can help these people lead full, normal lives. Examples include the wheelchair, artificial limbs, ramps in buildings and shopping centers, specially equipped cars, and eyeglasses.

Some pet owners in California searched for a way to help their deaf dogs and found a hearing aid service that had recently purchased a new invention especially for canines.

EXTENSIONS:

1. Have students think about a person with a physical handicap they may know or have seen. Let them invent something to make his/her life better.

2. Have students write for more information to:
The National Foundation for Crippled Children & Adults,
2023 W. Ogden Avenue
Chicago, Illinois 60612

SHAKE

LET THERE BE LIGHT!

Can you imagine what it would be like without electric lights?

INVENTION

Thomas Alva Edison is perhaps regarded as one of the greatest inventors in history. His inventions have had important effects on our lives. Some of his most famous were the electric light bulb, phonograph, and motion picture machine.

As a young boy, Edison read books. He had such a good memory, he rarely forgot any information. When Edison was only 9 years old, he decided to become an inventor. He sold newspapers to earn money to pay for the chemicals needed for his experiments.

Whenever Edison thought of an idea, he read everything he could find on the subject. He tested his ideas over and over until he was sure they might work.

Edison invented wax paper for wrapping food, and he invented a modern system of fire alarms. Sending several different telegraph messages over the same line was another of Edison's inventions. In 1877 he made improvements in Alexander Graham Bell's invention the telephone.

Edison was 84 years old when he died, and he had patents on more than 1,000 inventions.

EXTENSIONS:

1. Let students think of ways people had light before Edison invented the electric light bulb. Let them draw some different ways.

2. Have students write mystery stories. Titles might be: "The Light Bulb that Would Not Work," or "The Case of the Missing Record Player." Students should concentrate on the setting, characters, plot, and action.

- Remind them that all stories should have a beginning, middle, and end.

DESIGNERS

• Did you know jeans were invented for panhandlers? • When did the miniskirt come to America?

INVENTION

Blue jeans: Levi Strauss left Bavaria in 1847 and came to America. He was 17 years old and could barely speak English. He worked in his family's business selling housewares and cloth. When Levi heard about the Gold Rush in 1849, he could hardly wait to get to California to seek his fortune. He learned that men who panned for gold needed extremely durable pants that would not tear at the knees, so Levi made some overalls from the canvas cloth.

Soon, every prospector and railroad worker wanted Levi's pants. He opened a small shop in San Francisco and improved his product. He dyed the cloth indigo blue which became the **blue jeans we wear today.** In 1860 brass rivets (from a blacksmith's shop) were added to the pockets to make them strong.

Miniskirts: Mary Quant was born in London, England, in 1934. She invented the miniskirt which came to America in 1965. Girls of all ages wore this very brief, popular look in skirts and dresses as well. Mary Quant's designs sold in major stores all over the world. By mid-1970 the miniskirt was "out," and trousers for women were "in." Mary designed these, too, and her creations encouraged women to decide for themselves about fashion – long or short, etc.

EXTENSION:

1. Let students draw new concepts in fashion for men, women, and/or children. Let them share their designs with the class.

TOASTERS AND MORE

What is a lightning machine?

─ INVENTION ─

As a small boy in Germany, Charles Proteus Steinmetz tried experimenting with fire. His father knew how dangerous this was and made him promise never to light a match when he was alone. Math was Charles' favorite subject, and he studied very hard. Later he would use his math abilities to find the scientific secrets in the coils of copper wire, blocks of soft iron, and different kinds of electrical currents.

Charles came to America in 1890. He wondered how he could improve street lamps. Oil lamps were used for light, and these had to be lit each night by a "lamp lighter," a man who carried a very long candle.

Charles began to design practical electric machines. He worked for a small, new company named General Electric in Schenectady, New York.

Charles always wondered what caused thunder and lightning, and in 1921, he invented a lightning machine that could throw bolts of electricity. This led Charles to inventing ways of making lightning "harmless" which saved entire systems of power lines.

Charles Steinmetz is famous for developing the electric toothbrush, shaver, stove, washing machine, toaster, iron, air conditioner, and electric typewriter. All these operate on his invention of alternating current.

EXTENSION:

1. Have students discuss improvements on the inventions mentioned and how these improvements could be made.
(Example: A shaver that cannot cut you, a toaster that butters your toast, etc.)

COMPUTERS

What material was used for the first computer?

INVENTION

Your brain is like a computer; it can count, add, and subtract. Electronic computers are not as intelligent as you. They cannot think for themselves and have ideas like you, but the computer is an important invention that helps people keep track of things.

The earliest computer was probably made of stones. One stone in the sand was equal to one thing.

Two thousand years ago, wood and metal rods with beads in a frame was another computer called an Abacus. People all over the world used it to solve mathematical problems. It is still widely used in China.

In 1642, Blaise Pascal, a Frenchman, invented a new computer that used wheels instead of beads. This machine could add up to 999,999.99. It could also subtract. Each wheel had ten notches numbered zero to nine. Today, these wheels in an electric meter box tell how much electricity is used in a building. In an odometer in a car, the wheel tells how many miles have been traveled.

In the late 1700s, Joseph Jacquard, a Frenchman, invented a way to control the pattern on a weaving loom. By punching holes into paper cards, the loom knew what to do. This was not counting, so it was not a computer. But it gave Herman Hollerith, an American, an idea!

Hollerith invented a machine to take a Census, a way to count how many people live in the United States. His first cards held as much as 240 pieces of information such as age, address, and occupation. These punch cards made it possible to count and keep records on 60 million people. People began to realize the importance of the memory functions of a computer.

Charles Babbage, an English mathematician, developed the idea of a mechanical digital computer in the 1830s. He designed and tried to build a machine called an analytical engine. He never completed this machine, but many of his ideas are used today.

INVENTION cont.

In 1930, Vannevan Bush, an American electrical engineer, built the first analog computer. This was used in World War II to help aim antiaircraft guns.

In 1944, the first digital computer was completed by Howard Aiken, a Harvard University professor. In 1946, the first digital computer controlled by vacuum tubes was called ENIAC (Electronic Numerical Integrator and Computer).

John von Neumann, an American mathematician, developed the idea of storing programs in the computer's memory. The 1950s brought the first mass-produced computers, and "the computer age" was here to stay.

The power and capacity of computers are doubled every several years due to constant technological advancements. The costs of computers drop steadily so that more and more people can afford to own them. Exciting careers in the industry are open and available to explore. Are you interested?

EXTENSIONS:

1. Make a list of computer words such as disk files, megabytes, technology, digital, debugging, etc. Have a spelling contest.

2. Have students research the latest ways the telephone company uses a computer.

3. Write to NASA and ask about computer usage. Share the information with your class.

4. Let students design a robot on their computers or on paper to help them perform a task. Be sure to "program" the robot (give it data) so it will know what the students want it to do.

You Name It!

How do inventors decide what to name their inventions?

INVENTION

Scott Stillinger invented a bounceless ball and named it Koosh. He decided the name sounded right for this product. His ball is made of skinny pieces of rubber, and children and adults can invent many creative games to play with Koosh. A Koosh cannot roll, and it should not hurt anybody or break anything in the house because it is soft and lightweight. Football, golf, dodgeball, and tabletop tennis can be played with a Koosh.

Some inventors use their names in their inventions' names. (Examples: The Franklin Stove, Ford Automobiles, Bell Telephones.)

The word "television" describes what the invention does; "tele" is sound and "vision" is sight. George Eastman, inventor of the Kodak camera, chose Kodak because his favorite letter was "K." Some of the most popular products usually have names that begin with either **S**, **C**, **M**, **P**, **B**, **A**, or **T**. (Ask students to think of any that start with these letters.

EXTENSION:

1. When students try to name their inventions, let them first write a short description of it and what it does. This will help give them ideas of what to name their inventions. Short names seem to be remembered better.

58

COMBINATIONS

Can you name an invention from Japan?

── INVENTION ──

Japanese inventors have developed many products combining several ideas into one invention. Here are a few examples:

The "World's Greatest Ironing Board" comes with adjustable legs for uneven floors and wire shelves under the board to hold clothes.

A fusion business combines a gas station, a video sales and rental shop, an art gallery, and a used car lot. Another business combines a bookstore, bowling alley, and a noodles restaurant.

There are machines that dispense a combination of products in addition to candy and soda. They offer computer software, batteries, magazines, cassettes, etc.

EXTENSION:

1. Ask students what things they can combine to invent a useful product. Here are some suggestions for them to think about.

   - Piece of chalk and a chalkboard eraser.

   - Radio, beach towel, sunscreen, and umbrella.

   - Pen with a memory including different colors of ink and crayon.

   - Chair with music, video, massage, and food.

A New World

What would you do to change and improve the environment?

INVENTION

In December, 1989, eight people entered a new world. It is a structure called Biosphere II built in a desert area called the Oracle in Arizona. It is sealed off and self-contained covering 2.25 acres with seven ecological zones: an agricultural region, tropical forest, a 35 foot deep ocean, a marshland, savanna, desert, and a four-story apartment house where the people will live.

Inside the structure are 139 different kinds of plants, fish, birds, insects; 137 food crops, chickens, and goats. Two hummingbirds will pollinate the 3,200 growing flowers.

The people can communicate with the outside world, but this experiment will last two years. They will live in this system until 1991. Biosphere II is an invention to help us develop methods to build a clean, nearly perfect place.

EXTENSION:

1. Have students draw a large circle and divide it into countries and areas for land and water. Let them decide ways they would want to live. Have them label each part. Finally, have each student write a story about his new world.

INVENTION SCRAPBOOK

Do you know the stories about Tom Sawyer and Huckleberry Finn?

INVENTION

These stories were written by Mark Twain. But that was not his real name. It was Samuel Clemens, and in 1873 he wrote, "Be it known that I, Samuel L. Clemens, of Hartford, Connecticut, have invented certain new and useful improvements in scrap-books."

Samuel Clemens was a very clever man. One of his inventions was to use "sticky pages." Some of the pages were entirely covered with glue. This would make the scrapbook "self-pasting."

Today, we have various kinds of scrapbooks and methods to save photographs, drawings, and articles from papers and magazines. The peel-back album pages eliminate the need for glue or tape. Double-stick tape is less messy than paste. Rubber cement works well because mistakes rub off.

EXTENSIONS:

1. Let students make their own invention scrapbooks. Tell them to look for and save pictures and articles from newspapers and magazines about new inventions. Be sure they date each one. Years from now it will be interesting to see when something was invented and by whom. They may be able to find some of this material by checking the obituary section of the newspaper. Sometimes, the death of a famous inventor is noted and the background information is interesting.

2. Remind students to choose a big scrapbook! They will have a lot to put in it!

BIBLIOGRAPHY

Barbie Dolls & Collectibles by Sybil DeWein & Joan Ashabraner *Crown Publishing*, NY, 1987.

Beautiful Junk by Jon Madian, *Little*, Boston, 1968.

Building Your Own Toys by Sabine Lohf, *Children's Press*, Chicago, 1990.

Carolrhoda Creative Minds Books, Inc. Minneapolis, 1982.
A Pocketful of Goobers (George Washington Carver)
We'll Race You, Henry (Henry Ford)
What Do You Mean? (Noah Webster)
Author: Jeri Ferris

Computers by Karen Jacobsen, *Children's Press*, Chicago, 1987.

Creative Classroom by Kathryn Shoemaker, *Winston Press*, Minneapolis, 1980.

Decide and Design by Doris Spivack, *Kolbe Concepts*, Phoenix, 1980.

Dreamers & Doers/Inventors Who Changed Our World by Norman Richards, *Atheneum*, NY, 1984.

Eggplants and Elevators by James Meyers, *Hart Publishing Co.*, NY, 1978.

Famous Inventors & Their Inventions by Fletcher Pratt, *Random House*, NY, 1955.

Grand Constructions by Ceserani/Ventura, *Putnam*, NY, 1987.

Grandfather Tang's Story by Ann Tompert, *Crown Publishers*, NY, 1971.

Great Inventors & Discoveries by Donald Clarke, *Marshall Cavendish Pub.*, London, 1978.

101 Hand Puppets by Richard Cummings, *Van Rees Press*, NY, 1982.

How To Save The Planet by Billy Goodman, *Avon Books*, NY, 1990.

Invention Book by Steven Caney, *Workman Pub.*, NY, 1985.

Levi's by Ed Cray, *Simon & Schuster*, NY, 1981.

Louis Braille by Margaret Davidson, *Scholastic Inc.*, NY 1971.

Meet Benjamin Franklin by Maggi Scarf, *Random House*, NY, 1989.

Mothers of Invention by E. Vare & G. Hacek, *William Morrow*, NY, 1987.

Mousetraps and Muffling Cups by Kenneth Lasson, *Arbor House*, NY, 1986.

Oh, the Thinks you can Think! by Dr. Seuss, *Random House*, NY, 1975.

...BIBLIOGRAPHY

Playing Cards by Robert Tilley, *Mandarin Pub.*, Hong Kong, 1967.

Poor Richard's Almanac by Benjamin Franklin, *Blue Mt. Arts*, Boulder, 1975.

Recyclopedia by Robin Simons, *Houghton Mifflin*, Boston, 1976.

Robots in Fact & Fiction by Melvin Berger, *Franklin Watts*, NY, 1980.

50 Simple Things You Can Do To Save The Earth. *The Earth Works Group*
    Berkley, 1989.

Tangrams, Calif. State Dept. of Education, 1981.

The Time Machine by H. G. Wells, *Hogarth Press*, London, 1952.

Up Goes the Skyscrapers by Gail Gibbons, *Macmillan*, NY, 1986.

The Value of Creativity; The Story of Thomas Edison
    by Ann Donegan Johnson, *Random House*, NY, 1978.

The Way Things Work by David Macauly, *Houghton Mifflin*, NY, 1988.

A Weed is a Flower: The Life of George Washington Carver
    by Aliki Brandenberg, *Prentice Hall, Inc.*, Canada, 1981.

Weird & Wacky Inventions by Jim Murphy, *Crown*, NY, 1983.

What It Feels Like to be a Building by Forest Wilson,
    The Preservation Press, Washington, DC, 1988.

What The World Needs Now by Steven Johnson, *Ten Speed Press*,
    Berkeley, 1984.

Why Do Clocks Run Clockwise? by David Feldman, *Harper & Row*, NY, 1950.

Why I Built the Boogle House by Helen Palmer, *Random House*, 1964.

The Wizard of Waste Environmental Education Program SWRL Educational
    Research & Development, Los Alamitos, CA, 1979.